Tiitle:"Digital Crescendo: Mastering the Symphony of Facebook Marketing"

I0422195

subtitle:"Harmonizing Success: Navigating the MetaVerse, Influencer Alliances, and Global Diversity in the Dynamic Symphony of Facebook Marketing"

Author name : Md Sibgatulla

INDEX

Introduction:

Introduction:

Welcome to "Social Symphony: Mastering Facebook Marketing," your all-encompassing guide to navigating the intricate realm of Facebook marketing with precision and purpose. In this digital age, where social media has become a linchpin in the success of businesses, understanding and harnessing the potential of Facebook is paramount.

This e-book is not just a manual; it's your companion on a journey through the dynamic landscape of Facebook, exploring its features, unraveling its algorithms, and uncovering strategies that go beyond the conventional. Whether you're a seasoned marketer seeking to refine your approach or a newcomer eager to establish a formidable online presence, "Social Symphony" is crafted to cater to your needs.

Chapter 1: Understanding the Facebook Ecosystem

Welcome to the foundational chapter of "Social Symphony: Mastering Facebook Marketing." To effectively navigate the vast landscape of Facebook marketing, it is imperative to comprehend the intricate ecosystem that constitutes this powerful social media platform.

1.1 Anatomy of a Facebook Page:
A Facebook Page serves as the cornerstone of your online presence. It's not merely a virtual business card but a dynamic hub where businesses, brands, and public figures showcase their identity. Explore the essential components of a Facebook Page, including profile and cover photos, the about section, and tabs for various functionalities.

1.2 Unveiling the Power of Facebook Groups:

Beyond Pages, Facebook Groups emerge as dynamic communities where like-minded individuals gather. Understand the distinct advantages of creating or participating in groups, fostering engagement, and creating a sense of community around your brand or interests.

1.3 Demystifying the Algorithm: How Facebook Decides What to Show:

Facebook's algorithm plays a pivotal role in determining the content users see on their feeds. Delve into the intricacies of this algorithm, understanding factors such as relevance score, engagement history, and post timing. Uncover strategies to optimize your content for increased visibility and engagement.

1.4 Facebook Insights for Strategic Decisions:

Navigate the analytical landscape of Facebook with the Insights tool. Gain valuable data on your audience, content performance, and engagement metrics. Learn how to interpret these insights to refine your strategy, tailor content to your audience, and make informed decisions for optimal results.

In mastering the intricacies of the Facebook ecosystem, you lay the groundwork for a successful marketing symphony. As you proceed through "Social Symphony," these foundational insights will serve as a compass, guiding you through the diverse strategies and tactics that follow.

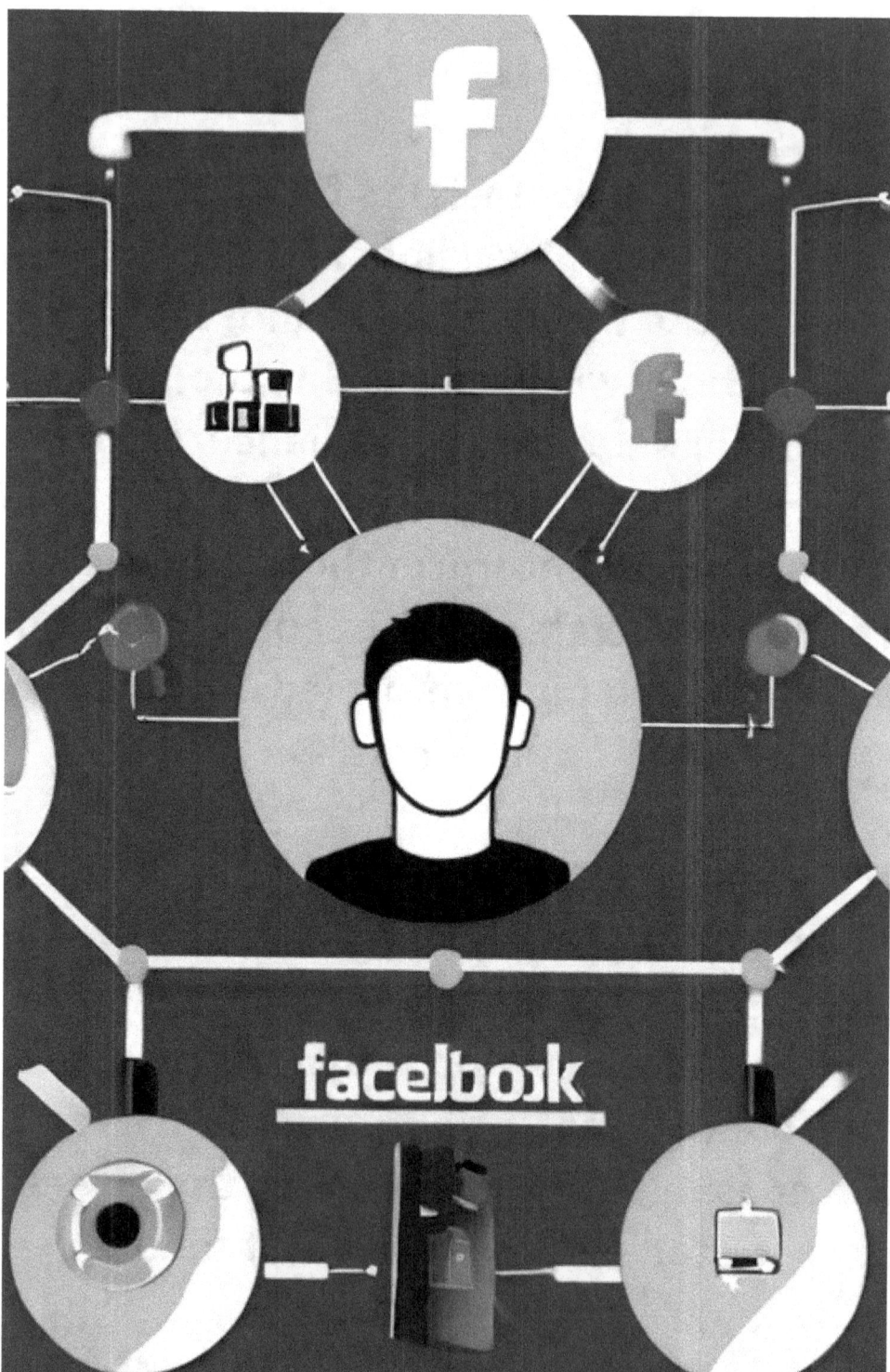

Chapter 2: Crafting a Compelling Brand Presence

In the symphony of Facebook marketing, creating a compelling brand presence is akin to composing the first notes of a memorable melody. This chapter delves into the art and science of presenting your brand on Facebook with resonance and impact.

2.1 Designing an Eye-Catching Profile and Cover Photo:

Your profile and cover photos are the visual overture to your brand. Learn the principles of designing visually appealing and on-brand images that capture attention and convey the essence of your business or persona.

2.2 Writing Engaging and Shareable Content:
Words have the power to inspire, inform, and ignite action. Explore the art of crafting compelling captions, status updates, and stories. Understand the psychology of shareable content, creating posts that resonate with your audience and prompt them to engage.

2.3 Leveraging Facebook Insights for Strategic Decisions:
Building on insights introduced in Chapter 1, delve deeper into using Facebook Insights specifically for crafting your brand's narrative. Identify content trends, understand audience preferences, and refine your messaging to align with your brand's goals.

As you embark on this journey of crafting a compelling brand presence, remember that authenticity and consistency are the keynotes. Your Facebook Page is not just a digital storefront; it's an invitation to engage with your brand. By understanding the nuances of design, language, and strategic decision-making, you lay the foundation for a harmonious brand symphony on Facebook.

In the vast landscape of Facebook marketing, success hinges on your ability to connect with the right audience. This chapter delves into the intricacies of building a targeted audience, ensuring that your content reaches the individuals most likely to resonate with your brand.

3.1 Utilizing Facebook Ads Manager Effectively:

Facebook Ads Manager is a powerful tool for creating and managing advertising campaigns. Explore the functionalities of Ads Manager, from creating ad sets to defining campaign objectives. Understand how to allocate budgets, schedule ads, and optimize for your specific marketing goals.

3.2 Creating Custom and Lookalike Audiences:

Tailor your outreach by harnessing the potential of custom audiences. Learn how to segment your existing audience based on factors such as demographics, interests, and behaviors. Additionally, discover the value of lookalike audiences, allowing Facebook to identify and target users similar to your existing customer base.

3.3 The Art of Ad Targeting: Demographics, Interests, and Behaviors:

Crafting targeted ads involves a nuanced understanding of your audience. Delve into the three pillars of ad targeting: demographics, interests, and behaviors. Explore how to leverage these categories to refine your audience targeting, ensuring your content reaches those most likely to engage and convert.

.

By mastering the art of building a targeted audience, you lay the groundwork for more meaningful interactions and higher conversion rates. As you proceed through the chapters of "Social Symphony," the insights gained here will prove instrumental in orchestrating a Facebook marketing strategy that resonates with the right audience

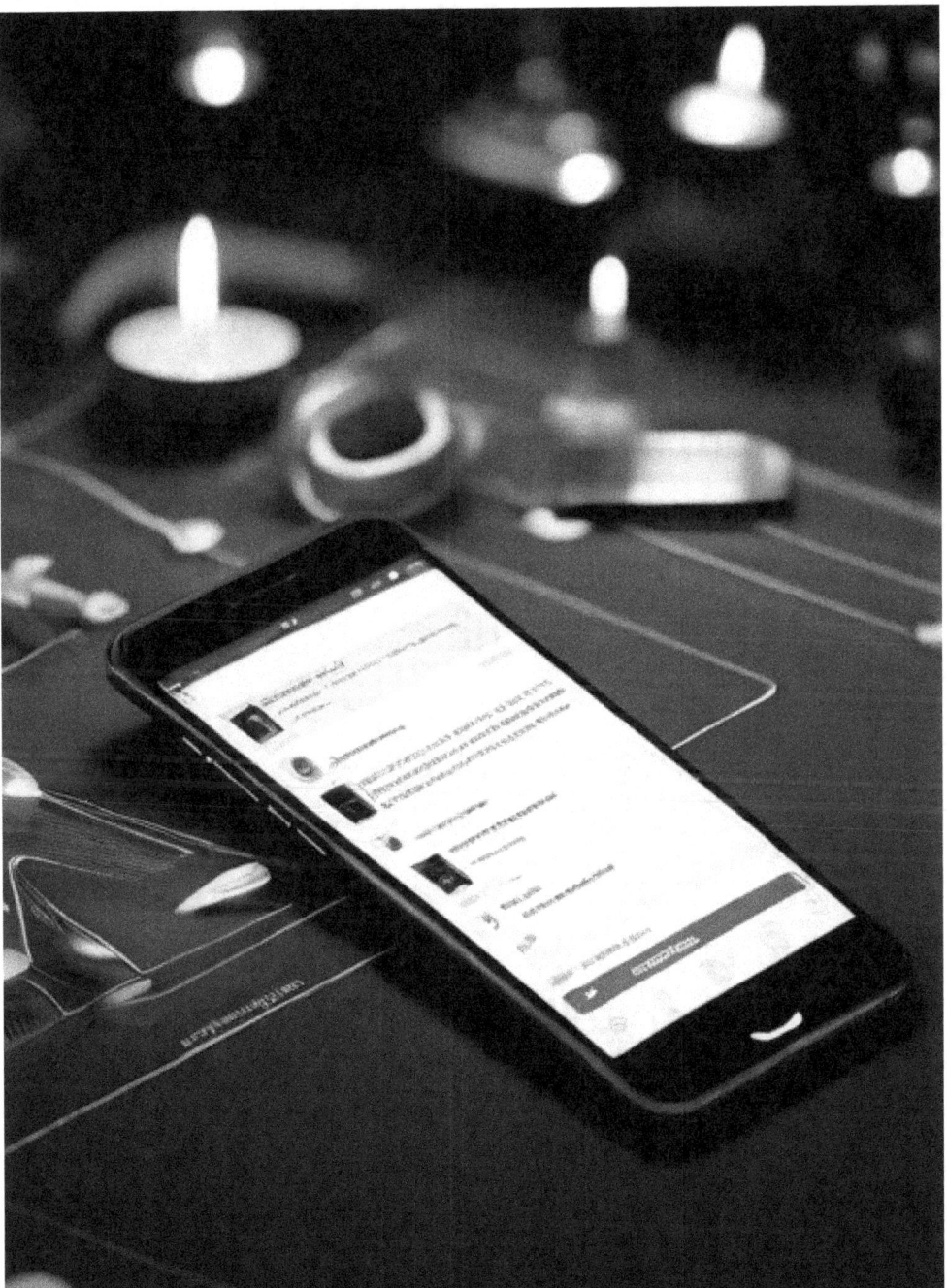

Chapter 4: Content that Converts

In the symphony of Facebook marketing, content is the melody that resonates with your audience, prompting engagement and conversion. This chapter unravels the art of crafting content that not only captures attention but also leads to meaningful actions.

4.1 The Importance of Storytelling in Facebook Marketing:

Great marketing transcends mere transactions; it tells a story. Understand the power of storytelling and how it creates an emotional connection with your audience. Learn to weave narratives that align with your brand, fostering a sense of identity and loyalty among your followers.

4.2 Types of Content that Resonate: Images, Videos, and Text:

Diversify your content portfolio by exploring the three main mediums on Facebook: images, videos, and text. Uncover the strengths of each format and discover how to leverage them to convey your message effectively. From visually compelling images to engaging video content, find the balance that suits your brand's narrative.

4.3 Strategies for Creating Shareable and Viral Content:

The true power of content lies in its shareability. Explore strategies for creating content that not only resonates with your existing audience but also compels them to share it with their networks. Uncover the elements that contribute to virality and learn how to amplify your reach through the social graph.

.

As you navigate the nuances of content creation, remember that quality triumphs over quantity. Each piece of content should contribute to the overall symphony of your brand, resonating with your audience and encouraging them to become active participants in your narrative

In the intricate dance of Facebook marketing, engagement is the heartbeat that sustains your brand's presence and relevance. This chapter unravels the strategies and techniques necessary for maximizing engagement, transforming passive viewers into active participants in your brand's symphony.

5.1 The Science of Timing: Best Times to Post on Facebook:

Timing is an often overlooked but crucial aspect of engagement. Explore the science behind determining the best times to post on Facebook. Understand the nuances of your audience's behavior, time zones, and daily routines to ensure your content reaches them when they are most receptive.

5.2 Techniques to Boost Likes, Comments, and Shares:

Likes, comments, and shares are the currency of engagement on Facebook. Discover proven techniques to encourage these interactions. From crafting compelling calls-to-action to asking questions that spark conversation, uncover strategies that elicit active engagement from your audience.

5.3 Running Successful Facebook Contests and Giveaways:

Contests and giveaways present exciting opportunities to amplify engagement. Learn the art of designing and executing successful Facebook contests. From defining clear objectives to promoting your contests effectively, discover how to leverage these events to increase brand visibility and foster a sense of community.

As you delve into the realm of maximizing engagement, remember that authenticity and relevance are the keys to creating a meaningful connection with your audience. The goal is not just interaction but building a community that actively participates in the narrative you're weaving.

Chapter 6: Harnessing the Power of Facebook Groups

In the symphony of social media, Facebook Groups emerge as a unique and dynamic instrument, allowing businesses, brands, and communities to create a harmonious space for engagement. This chapter unravels the potential of Facebook Groups and provides insights into effectively harnessing their power.

6.1 Building and Managing a Thriving Facebook Group:

Facebook Groups provide a dedicated space for like-minded individuals to connect, share, and engage. Understand the principles of creating and managing a thriving group. From defining the group's purpose to establishing guidelines for participation, learn how to foster a vibrant community.

6.2 Strategies for Community Engagement:

The essence of a successful Facebook Group lies in active community engagement. Explore strategies to encourage discussions, facilitate member interactions, and create a sense of belonging. From regular prompts to themed discussions, uncover techniques to keep your group dynamic and engaged.

6.3 Monetizing Facebook Groups Without Alienating Members:

For businesses, the question of monetization often arises. Discover ethical and effective ways to monetize your Facebook Group without compromising its integrity. From offering exclusive content to strategic partnerships, explore avenues that add value to both your brand and your group members.

As you delve into the realm of Facebook Groups, remember that cultivating a sense of community is paramount. It's not just about broadcasting messages but creating a space where members actively participate, forging connections that extend beyond the digital realm.

In the symphony of Facebook marketing, analytics and measurement serve as the conductor, providing invaluable insights to refine your strategy and enhance performance. This chapter delves into the world of metrics, helping you decode the data to make informed decisions and fine-tune your brand's symphony.

7.1 Key Metrics to Track for Facebook Success:

Navigate the sea of metrics by identifying and understanding the key performance indicators (KPIs) that align with your goals. From reach and engagement to conversion metrics, learn how to measure success accurately and tailor your strategy accordingly.

7.2 Understanding Facebook Insights:
Facebook Insights is your orchestra's sheet music, providing a detailed score of your page's performance. Explore the features of Facebook Insights, deciphering data on audience demographics, post reach, and engagement. Understand how to leverage these insights to refine your content strategy.

7.3 A/B Testing for Continuous Improvement:
In the pursuit of perfection, A/B testing becomes your rehearsal studio. Learn the art of conducting experiments to compare different variables within your Facebook strategy. From ad creatives to posting times, uncover how A/B testing can lead to continuous improvement and optimization.

As you embark on this analytical journey, remember that data is not merely numbers but a symphony of insights waiting to be played. By mastering analytics and measurement, you gain the ability to refine your strategy, amplify your strengths, and harmonize your efforts for optimal results.

In the intricate symphony of Facebook marketing, unforeseen challenges may arise, requiring a carefully orchestrated response. This chapter delves into the art of crisis management on Facebook, guiding you on how to navigate difficult situations while maintaining the integrity of your brand's symphony.

8.1 Strategies for Handling Negative Comments and Reviews:
Negative comments and reviews can be dissonant notes in your brand's melody. Explore effective strategies for addressing criticism and negativity on your Facebook Page. Learn how to respond professionally, resolve issues transparently, and turn negative experiences into opportunities for positive engagement.

8.2 Turning Challenges into Opportunities:
Crisis moments can be transformative if approached with the right mindset. Understand how to turn challenges into opportunities for growth and improvement. Whether addressing a product issue or a public relations concern, discover how to navigate crises in a way that enhances your brand's reputation.

8.3 Developing a Proactive Social Media Crisis Plan:
Preparation is the key to effective crisis management. Develop a proactive social media crisis plan tailored to the unique challenges of Facebook. Outline roles and responsibilities, establish response protocols, and create a communication strategy to ensure a swift and coordinated response when facing unexpected crises.

As you delve into the realm of crisis management on Facebook, remember that resilience and transparency are the guiding principles. By addressing challenges with grace and learning from them, you not only preserve your brand's integrity but also contribute to the ongoing refinement of your marketing symphony.

In the dynamic orchestration of Facebook marketing, video content takes center stage as a powerful and immersive medium. This chapter delves into the strategies and techniques for leveraging Facebook Live and video marketing to captivate your audience and elevate your brand's symphony.

9.1 Mastering Facebook Live for Real-Time Engagement:

Facebook Live is your direct line to real-time audience engagement. Explore the nuances of going live on Facebook, from planning engaging sessions to interacting with viewers in real-time. Learn how to use this feature to humanize your brand, answer questions, and build a deeper connection with your audience.

9.2 Creating Impactful Videos for Your Audience:
Beyond live sessions, pre-recorded videos form the backbone of your video marketing strategy. Uncover the principles of creating impactful videos, from storytelling and scriptwriting to editing and optimizing for different platforms. Understand the importance of visual appeal, audio quality, and concise messaging.

9.3 Leveraging IGTV for Extended Reach:
Extend your video symphony to Instagram's IGTV, seamlessly integrating it into your Facebook strategy. Discover how IGTV complements your video content on Facebook, reaching a broader audience and tapping into the engaged user base of Instagram. Learn to repurpose and optimize your videos for IGTV.

As you delve into the realm of Facebook Live and video marketing, remember that authenticity and creativity are the instruments that resonate most with audiences. By incorporating video into your symphony, you not only showcase your brand in a compelling light but also offer an immersive experience that resonates deeply with your audience.

Chapter 10: Staying Ahead of Trends

In the ever-evolving symphony of Facebook marketing, staying ahead of trends is akin to conducting an orchestra with a keen ear for the latest harmonies. This chapter explores the importance of trend-spotting and provides strategies to ensure that your brand's symphony remains fresh, relevant, and resonant.

10.1 The Evolving Landscape of Facebook and Social Media:
Understand that the only constant in the digital realm is change. Explore the dynamic shifts in the landscape of Facebook and social media. Stay abreast of platform updates, algorithm changes, and emerging features that could impact your marketing strategy.

10.2 Emerging Trends in Facebook Marketing:
Identify and embrace the emerging trends shaping the future of Facebook marketing. Whether it's the rise of new content formats, changes in user behavior, or innovative ad features, staying informed about these trends allows you to adapt and integrate them seamlessly into your strategy.

10.3 Adapting and Staying Competitive:
Adaptability is the key to longevity in the world of Facebook marketing. Learn how to pivot and adjust your strategies based on evolving trends. Explore case studies of brands that successfully navigated changes in the digital landscape, and extract valuable lessons for your own orchestration.

As you navigate the dynamic terrain of trends, remember that innovation is the heartbeat of success. By embracing change, monitoring emerging trends, and adapting your symphony accordingly, you position your brand not just to keep pace but to lead the evolving narrative of Facebook marketing.

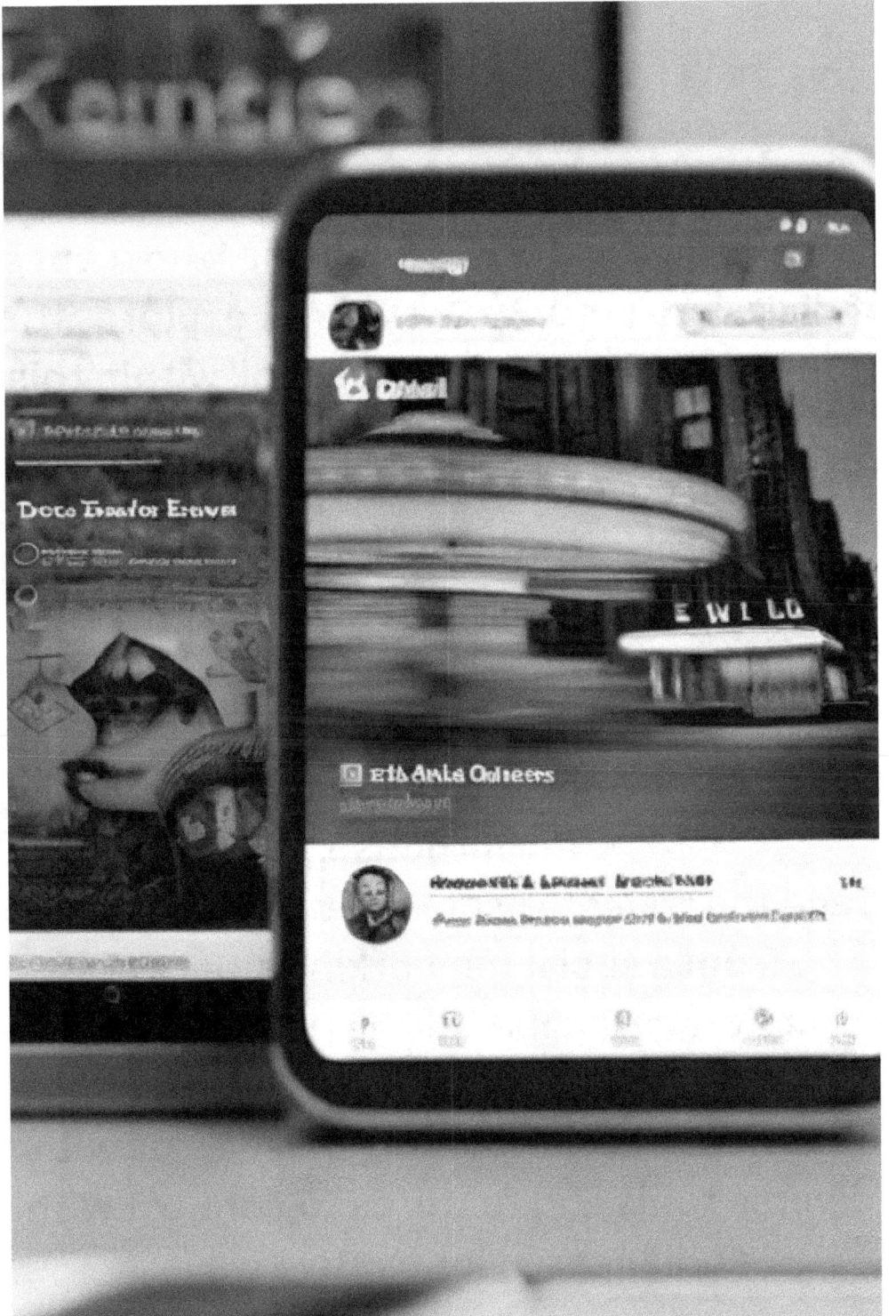

Chapter 11: The Evolving Role of Facebook in Digital Marketing

As we navigate the ever-shifting landscapes of digital marketing, Chapter 11 explores the transformative role of Facebook within this dynamic ecosystem. Understanding how Facebook evolves and adapts is essential for orchestrating a symphony that resonates with the contemporary rhythms of online engagement.

11.1 From Social Network to Marketing Powerhouse:

Trace the trajectory of Facebook's evolution from a social networking site to a multifaceted marketing powerhouse. Explore how the platform has expanded its functionalities, providing businesses with diverse tools and features to connect with audiences in innovative ways.

11.2 Adapting to User Behavior and Expectations:

User behavior shapes the digital landscape, and Facebook has demonstrated a remarkable ability to adapt to changing user expectations. Understand how the platform aligns itself with evolving user behaviors, preferences, and expectations, allowing marketers to stay relevant in their strategies.

11.3 Integration of E-Commerce and Social Commerce:

Witness the integration of e-commerce and social commerce within the Facebook ecosystem. Explore how businesses can leverage features like Facebook Shops and seamless integration with online marketplaces to create a unified and engaging shopping experience for users.

11.4 Facebook as a Content Discovery Platform:

Recognize the role of Facebook as a content discovery platform. Explore how users discover, consume, and engage with diverse content on the platform, and understand the implications for content creators and marketers aiming to capture attention in an information-rich environment.

11.5 Cross-Platform Integration and the Meta Transition:

Dive into the concept of cross-platform integration and the broader transition into the metaverse under Meta. Explore the implications of this transition for digital marketing and how businesses can prepare for a future where online experiences transcend traditional boundaries.

In this chapter, we unravel the intricate threads that weave Facebook into the fabric of modern digital marketing. By understanding its evolving role, marketers can adapt their strategies to leverage the platform's full potential, ensuring their symphony resonates with the contemporary audience.

Chapter 12: Beyond Likes: Measuring Real Engagement

In the orchestration of a successful Facebook marketing symphony, Chapter 12 transcends the superficial metric of likes and delves into the realm of measuring real engagement. Understanding that meaningful interactions are the true melody of success, this chapter explores strategies to gauge and enhance the depth of audience engagement on the platform.

12.1 Defining Real Engagement:
Likes, while valuable, are just the tip of the iceberg. Define what real engagement means for your brand. It could encompass comments, shares, click-throughs, and other actions that indicate a deeper connection with your content.

12.2 Deciphering Comments and Conversations:

Comments are a direct line to understanding your audience's thoughts and sentiments. Learn how to decipher comments, fostering meaningful conversations that go beyond mere acknowledgment. Discover strategies to encourage dialogue and respond effectively to audience input.

12.3 Encouraging Shares for Amplified Reach:

Shares are the currency of organic reach on Facebook. Uncover techniques to encourage users to share your content. From creating shareable visuals to crafting content that resonates emotionally, learn how to transform your audience into ambassadors who willingly broadcast your brand message.

12.4 Click-Throughs and Conversion Metrics: Measure engagement beyond the platform by tracking click-throughs and conversion metrics. Understand the journey users take from Facebook to your website or landing pages. Utilize analytics to assess the effectiveness of your content in driving actions beyond the social media realm.

12.5 Analyzing Video Engagement Metrics: For video content, delve into specialized metrics like watch time, completion rates, and audience retention. Understand how viewers interact with your videos and optimize your content to keep audiences captivated from start to finish.

By navigating beyond the superficial allure of likes and prioritizing real engagement metrics, marketers can compose a symphony that not only attracts attention but also cultivates a community of active and committed participants in the narrative of the brand.

In the evolution of Facebook marketing, the symphony of advertisements takes on new dimensions with advanced ad formats. Chapter 13 delves into the intricacies of three powerful formats—Carousel, Collection, and Canvas—offering insights on how to orchestrate captivating campaigns that resonate with your audience.

13.1 Carousel Ads: A Dynamic Storytelling Experience:

Carousel ads allow advertisers to tell a visual story in a dynamic and interactive format. Learn how to leverage multiple images or videos within a single ad unit, guiding your audience through a narrative that captures attention and encourages exploration.

13.2 Collection Ads: Showcasing Products in a Seamless Experience:

For e-commerce businesses, Collection ads offer a seamless shopping experience within the Facebook platform. Explore how to curate visually appealing collections of products, providing users with a cohesive and immersive browsing experience that seamlessly transitions to a shopping journey.

13.3 Canvas Ads: Immersive Brand Experiences:

Canvas ads invite users into an immersive, full-screen experience designed to captivate and engage. Understand how to craft Canvas ads that go beyond traditional formats, using interactive elements, storytelling, and multimedia to create an unforgettable brand experience directly within the Facebook platform.

13.4 Tailoring Ad Content for Different Objectives:

Each advanced ad format serves unique objectives. Learn how to tailor your content to suit specific campaign goals, whether it's driving awareness, encouraging product discovery, or fostering brand engagement. Understanding the nuances of each format allows you to select the right tool for the job.

13.5 Optimization Techniques for Advanced Ads:

Optimization is crucial for the success of advanced ad campaigns. Explore techniques for optimizing visuals, copy, and targeting to maximize the impact of your Carousel, Collection, and Canvas ads. Understand how to analyze performance metrics and iterate on your strategy for continuous improvement.

As you venture into the realm of advanced ad strategies, remember that these formats offer a symphony of creative possibilities. By mastering Carousel, Collection, and Canvas ads, you elevate your advertising orchestration, creating campaigns that not only capture attention but also immerse your audience in a rich and memorable brand experience.

Chapter 14: The Rise of Messenger Marketing

In the dynamic landscape of Facebook marketing, Chapter 14 explores the ascendancy of Messenger Marketing as a powerful and personalized communication channel. This chapter unravels the strategies and insights behind leveraging Facebook Messenger to create meaningful connections with your audience.

14.1 The Evolution of Messaging Platforms: Messaging platforms have evolved from simple communication tools to multifaceted ecosystems. Understand how Facebook Messenger has emerged as a central hub for personalized interactions, blurring the lines between communication and marketing.

14.2 Leveraging Chatbots for Automation:
Explore the integration of chatbots within Messenger, enabling businesses to automate responses, streamline customer interactions, and provide instant support. Learn how to design and deploy chatbots that enhance user experiences and guide users through predefined interactions.

14.3 Personalized Conversations and User Engagement:
Messenger Marketing allows for highly personalized conversations. Dive into strategies for engaging users on an individual level, delivering tailored content, and facilitating seamless transactions. Understand the importance of creating conversational experiences that feel authentic and human.

14.4 Building Subscriber Lists and Growing Audiences:

Messenger enables businesses to build subscriber lists, creating a direct line of communication with interested users. Explore techniques for growing Messenger audiences, from strategic opt-in processes to promoting exclusive content and offers that incentivize users to subscribe.

14.5 Adapting to Messaging Trends and Privacy Concerns:

Stay abreast of evolving messaging trends and navigate privacy concerns effectively. Understand the importance of balancing personalized communication with user privacy, and adapt your Messenger Marketing strategy in response to changing user expectations and regulatory environments.

By embracing the rise of Messenger Marketing, businesses can forge deeper connections with their audience, offering a personalized and interactive experience that transcends traditional marketing channels. As you explore the potential of Messenger, remember that building genuine relationships through meaningful conversations is the heartbeat of this innovative approach.

Chapter 15: Integrating Instagram into Your Facebook Strategy

As the symphony of social media continues to harmonize, Chapter 15 explores the seamless integration of Instagram into your broader Facebook marketing strategy. This chapter delves into the interconnected worlds of these platforms, offering insights on how to leverage Instagram to amplify your brand's narrative.

15.1 Understanding the Symbiotic Relationship:

Recognize the symbiotic relationship between Facebook and Instagram, both owned by Meta. Understand how these platforms complement each other, catering to diverse audience demographics and offering unique features for content delivery.

15.2 Seamless Cross-Posting and Cross-Promotion:
Explore strategies for cross-posting content between Facebook and Instagram. Learn how to tailor your posts for each platform while maintaining a consistent brand voice. Understand the nuances of cross-promotion to maximize visibility and engagement across both platforms.

15.3 Leveraging Instagram Stories and Reels:
Instagram's dynamic features, Stories and Reels, offer unique opportunities for creative expression. Dive into techniques for integrating these formats into your overall content strategy. Learn how to craft engaging and shareable content that aligns with your brand's narrative.

15.4 Running Unified Ad Campaigns:
Unify your advertising efforts by running campaigns across both platforms through Ads Manager. Understand how to leverage the targeting capabilities of both Facebook and Instagram to reach specific audiences. Explore the nuances of ad formats that resonate effectively on each platform.

15.5 Tailoring Content for Instagram's Visual Appeal:
Instagram's visual-centric nature demands a tailored approach to content creation. Discover how to optimize your visuals, use Instagram's unique filters, and harness the power of visually appealing content to captivate your audience.

By integrating Instagram into your Facebook strategy, you create a harmonious melody that resonates across diverse audiences. As you navigate the interconnected worlds of these platforms, remember that a cohesive and integrated approach enhances your brand's presence, forging a unified narrative that captivates users on both Facebook and Instagram.

In the ever-evolving landscape of digital marketing, Chapter 16 addresses the paramount importance of adhering to privacy regulations, with a specific focus on the General Data Protection Regulation (GDPR) and related privacy concerns in the context of Facebook marketing.

16.1 The Significance of GDPR in Marketing: Understand the foundational principles of GDPR and how it reshapes the landscape of data protection and user privacy. Explore the rights bestowed upon individuals and the obligations placed on businesses when processing personal data, emphasizing transparency and user consent.

16.2 Implications for Facebook Marketing Practices:

Delve into the implications of GDPR for Facebook marketing practices. Learn how the regulation affects the collection, processing, and storage of user data on the platform. Explore strategies for ensuring compliance while still delivering effective and personalized marketing experiences.

16.3 Consent Mechanisms and Opt-In Strategies:

Uncover effective consent mechanisms and opt-in strategies to navigate GDPR requirements within the Facebook ecosystem. Explore how to obtain clear and unambiguous consent from users, ensuring that they have control over how their data is used for marketing purposes.

16.4 Data Security and Handling:
Address the critical aspect of data security within the realm of Facebook marketing. Understand the measures required to secure user data, prevent breaches, and respond effectively in the event of a data security incident. Compliance with GDPR involves not only consent but also robust data protection measures.

16.5 Privacy by Design:
Embrace the concept of privacy by design in your Facebook marketing strategy. Explore how to integrate privacy considerations from the inception of your campaigns, ensuring that user privacy is prioritized at every stage of the marketing process.

As privacy concerns become increasingly central to the digital marketing landscape, navigating the nuances of GDPR in the context of Facebook marketing is not just a legal requirement but a commitment to building trust with your audience. By adopting privacy-conscious practices, businesses can navigate the regulatory landscape while delivering personalized and respectful marketing experiences.

In the symphony of Facebook marketing, Chapter 17 explores the art and strategy behind leveraging influencer marketing—a powerful approach that involves collaborating with influential individuals to amplify your brand's reach and credibility on the platform.

17.1 Understanding Influencer Marketing Dynamics:

Delve into the dynamics of influencer marketing and how it has become a significant force on Facebook. Understand the role influencers play in connecting with audiences, building trust, and driving engagement through authentic and relatable content.

17.2 Identifying the Right Influencers for Your Brand:

Choosing the right influencers is pivotal to the success of your influencer marketing campaign. Explore strategies for identifying influencers whose values align with your brand, and whose audience demographics match your target market. Consider factors such as engagement rates, authenticity, and relevance.

17.3 Crafting Effective Influencer Campaigns:

Learn the art of designing influencer campaigns that resonate with your audience. From defining campaign goals and key performance indicators to establishing clear collaboration guidelines, discover how to orchestrate campaigns that seamlessly integrate influencers into your brand's narrative.

17.4 Navigating Disclosure and Transparency:
Navigate the landscape of disclosure and transparency in influencer marketing. Understand the legal and ethical considerations surrounding sponsored content, and explore effective ways to ensure that influencer partnerships are transparently communicated to the audience.

17.5 Measuring Influencer Marketing ROI: Dive into the metrics and key performance indicators (KPIs) used to measure the return on investment (ROI) of influencer marketing on Facebook. Explore how to assess the impact of influencer campaigns on brand awareness, engagement, and conversions, allowing you to refine your strategies for future collaborations.

By mastering the art of influencer marketing on Facebook, businesses can tap into the authentic and influential voices that resonate with their target audience. The result is a harmonious collaboration that not only expands reach but also cultivates trust and credibility in the ever-evolving symphony of digital marketing.

Chapter 18: Diversifying Content for Global Audiences

In the expansive realm of Facebook marketing, Chapter 18 unravels the essential strategies for diversifying content to resonate with diverse global audiences. Navigating the nuances of cultural variations, languages, and preferences, this chapter guides marketers in crafting a symphony that transcends borders.

18.1 Embracing Cultural Sensitivity: Cultural sensitivity is the cornerstone of successfully engaging global audiences. Explore the importance of understanding cultural nuances, customs, and sensitivities to ensure that your content resonates positively and avoids unintentional misunderstandings.

18.2 Multilingual Content Strategies:
Adapt your content to the linguistic diversity of your global audience. Learn effective strategies for incorporating multiple languages into your content, from multilingual posts to language-specific campaigns. This approach ensures that language barriers do not hinder the global reach of your brand.

18.3 Localization Techniques for Visual Content:
Visual content speaks a universal language, but nuances in design and imagery can impact interpretation. Explore localization techniques for visual content, ensuring that graphics, images, and videos are culturally relevant and resonate with audiences from different regions.

18.4 Tailoring Messaging to Regional Preferences:
Messaging preferences vary across regions. Discover how to tailor your messaging to align with regional preferences and communication styles. Whether it's humor, formality, or the use of specific idioms, adapting your tone ensures that your content feels familiar and relatable to diverse audiences.

18.5 Timing and Cultural Calendar Considerations:
Consider the timing of your content in relation to cultural calendars and events. Explore how aligning your content schedule with regional holidays, festivals, and significant events can enhance relevance and engagement with audiences around the world.

By diversifying content for global audiences, businesses can create a harmonious symphony that transcends cultural boundaries. The art lies in crafting messages that are not only linguistically accessible but also culturally resonant, fostering a connection that goes beyond geographical borders.

In the ever-evolving landscape of Facebook marketing, Chapter 19 ventures into the frontier of future trends, with a specific focus on Meta—the parent company of Facebook—and the emerging concept of the metaverse. This chapter unravels the transformative implications of these trends on the future symphony of digital marketing.

19.1 Meta's Vision and Rebranding: Explore Meta's visionary rebranding and the company's mission to create a more connected and immersive online experience. Understand the strategic shift from being primarily a social media company to focusing on building the metaverse—a collective virtual shared space that blurs the line between physical and digital realities.

19.2 The Metaverse and Its Impact on Digital Interaction:

Dive into the concept of the metaverse as a new frontier for digital interaction. Understand how the metaverse envisions a seamless blend of virtual and physical experiences, opening up unprecedented opportunities for businesses to engage with audiences in immersive and interactive ways.

19.3 Implications for Social Media and Marketing:

Examine the implications of the metaverse for social media and marketing strategies. Explore how businesses can leverage this evolving landscape to create novel and engaging experiences for users. From virtual storefronts to immersive brand interactions, discover the potential for marketing campaigns within the metaverse.

19.4 Augmented and Virtual Reality Experiences:

Augmented Reality (AR) and Virtual Reality (VR) are integral to the metaverse experience. Learn about the potential applications of AR and VR in marketing, including virtual try-ons, interactive product demonstrations, and immersive brand storytelling. Understand how these technologies can elevate user engagement.

19.5 Adapting Strategies for the Metaverse Era:

As the metaverse era dawns, businesses need to adapt their marketing strategies. Explore proactive steps to prepare for the metaverse, including staying informed about emerging technologies, experimenting with virtual experiences, and envisioning innovative ways to connect with audiences in this evolving digital landscape.

By exploring the future trends of Meta and the metaverse, businesses can position themselves at the forefront of digital innovation. The metaverse represents not only a shift in technology but also a new frontier for creativity, collaboration, and immersive brand experiences, shaping the future symphony of Facebook marketing.

Chapter 20: Your Journey Continues: Staying Agile in the Digital Age

As we conclude this symphony of insights into Facebook marketing, Chapter 20 serves as a guide for marketers to navigate the ever-evolving digital landscape with agility and adaptability. In the fast-paced and dynamic world of online engagement, staying agile is the key to sustained success.

20.1 Embracing Continuous Learning: The digital age is characterized by rapid advancements and constant innovation. Cultivate a mindset of continuous learning to stay abreast of emerging trends, tools, and technologies. Engage in industry forums, attend webinars, and invest in ongoing education to evolve with the digital landscape.

20.2 Agility in Response to Algorithm Changes:

Facebook's algorithms, like any technology, are subject to change. Stay agile in response to algorithm updates by monitoring industry news and adapting your strategies accordingly. Flexibility and a willingness to adjust your approach are crucial in navigating the nuances of algorithmic shifts.

20.3 Experimenting with New Features and Formats:

Digital platforms frequently introduce new features and content formats. Embrace a culture of experimentation by testing these features to understand their impact on your audience. Whether it's exploring new ad formats or diving into emerging trends, experimenting allows you to discover what resonates best with your audience.

20.4 Fostering a Culture of Innovation:
Innovation is a driving force in the digital age. Foster a culture of innovation within your team or organization. Encourage creative thinking, cross-functional collaboration, and a willingness to explore unconventional approaches. Innovation often arises from a diversity of perspectives and a willingness to challenge the status quo.

20.5 Building Resilience in the Face of Challenges:
The digital landscape is not without challenges. From algorithm changes to crises, building resilience is essential. Develop strategies for crisis management, establish contingency plans, and foster a resilient mindset that allows your brand to navigate uncertainties with grace and adaptability.

As your journey in the digital age continues, remember that agility is not just a response to change but a proactive stance toward growth and evolution. By embracing continuous learning, adapting to changes, experimenting with new possibilities, fostering innovation, and building resilience, you equip yourself to orchestrate a dynamic and successful symphony in the ever-evolving world of Facebook marketing.

Conclusion: Orchestrating Success in the Facebook Symphony

In this comprehensive exploration of Facebook marketing, we've traversed the diverse movements and harmonies that constitute a successful symphony in the digital age. From understanding the intricacies of the Facebook ecosystem to delving into advanced ad strategies, influencer marketing, and the promising realms of Meta and the metaverse, each chapter has contributed to a nuanced understanding of the multifaceted landscape.

As the conductor of your brand's symphony, it's crucial to recognize that Facebook marketing is not a static composition; it's a dynamic and ever-evolving orchestration that requires continuous learning, adaptability, and a keen ear for emerging trends. The symphony isn't confined to the familiar notes of today but extends into the uncharted melodies of tomorrow.

The future of Facebook marketing is intertwined with technological advancements, user behaviors, and the transformative vision of Meta in building the metaverse. Navigating this landscape requires not only strategic acumen but also an openness to experimentation, a commitment to ethical practices, and a deep understanding of your audience's evolving expectations.

In the digital age, success isn't solely measured by metrics but by the resonance of your symphony with the hearts and minds of your audience. From crafting compelling brand stories to navigating privacy concerns, from embracing cultural diversity to anticipating the trends of the metaverse, your journey as a digital conductor is a perpetual evolution.

As you move forward, remember that the symphony of Facebook marketing is not just about the brand; it's about the community you build, the conversations you spark, and the connections you forge. It's about creating an immersive and memorable experience that transcends the boundaries of the digital realm.

The chapters of this book have provided you with the sheet music, but the orchestration is in your hands. Stay agile, embrace innovation, and continue refining your symphony. As you embark on the next movements of your Facebook marketing journey, may your brand's melody resonate far and wide in the ever-expanding digital symphony.

Conduct with passion, adapt with grace, and let your symphony echo through the digital corridors of success.

[Author Name]

Md sibgatulla

www.ingramcontent.com/pod-product-compliance
Lightning Source LLC
Chambersburg PA
CBHW071157290526
45796CB00007B/64